More than Just a *Pretty* Smile

A Book Collaboration By:
Kelly Y. Ragin & Nedra Ford

3G Publishing, Inc.
Loganville, Ga 30052
www.3gpublishinginc.com
Phone: 1-888-442-9637

First published by 3G Publishing, Inc. June, 2020

ISBN: 978-1-941247-73-0

Printed in the United States of America

Contents

Acknowledgements

There's so much to write when it comes to expressing my gratitude. Sometimes, it feels as though there's not enough space or time to do so. However, as with everything, I give honor to God first who has gifted my mind and my hands to serve in the capacity of writing. He has used my life in many ways to serve as an example for others which leads me to share my journey through written expression----and for this, I say THANK YOU.

I also want to thank *my family and friends* who have supported me along the way. It's unbelievable to know how strong my back support is and I owe it to my tribe. I LOVE YOU ALL!!

To my awesome book cover designers *Briyanna Ruff* and *Ericka Robinson*—thank you! Briyanna---you captured the pretty side of the title at the first try! I fell in love with it instantly. Ericka, my daughter—thank you for your talent in adding the finishing touch! And *Erin-*--your eagle eye is always on point. What would I do without you two?

To *my mother, Ms. Linda Stepp*, there are never enough words, so I hope that you smile each time I present you with a new copy of a published book from your "little girl" who learned to love reading because of you.
I love you Mama!

To my best friend. My life partner. My biggest fan,
and the love of my life, THANK YOU. For years, as
my solid friend, you've always supported me. You've
always shown up. You've always spread the good news
on my behalf. And you've always believed in me. I will
never forget that one year when you called me (wayyy
before you became my sweetie. Lol) and you said…
"Kelly—keep doing what you're doing. Remember that
somebody is always watching you and you're doing
a great job. Don't quit". Those words will always be
etched on my heart. Thank you for loving me….
REALLY loving me. It makes it easy to love you back. *I
Love you Perry.*

Introduction

Often, after sharing my personal stories of challenge and triumph, I've heard people say, "WOW! You sure don't look like what you've been through. "For this, I'm grateful, but I know I'm just one person out of millions who can attest to these same sentiments. This truly puts things into perspective for me. Why? Because it forces me to reflect on all that I've gone through. My life's journey.

My Story.

More Than Just a Pretty Smile is a book collaboration. This is actually the first volume of many. Hopefully, you as our beloved readers, will be engaged, encouraged and empowered! This is the only purpose. Many times, we as women go through life battling and struggling with some serious real-life issues. The kind of issues that we feel no one in this entire world would ever understand. The kind of issues that are deep rooted and tucked away never to surface (or so we think). The kind of issues that have demons of despair, depression, hurt and pain. Well there's GOOD NEWS! There's hope!

More Than Just a Pretty Smile is here to the rescue! Please allow our testimonies and words of revelation and encouragement to uplift your soul.

We are here to serve.
-Kelly

More Than Just A Pretty Smile

This title means so much to me. Someone recently asked me how did I choose this title. It really made me reflect on where I was in my life during this time. I recall attending an event and ran into an old friend. She had recently gone through a divorce and began to share some of her struggles.

At that time, she teasingly said to me, "Kelly, I need you to give a class on flirting. You never ever seemed to have had a problem with getting a man's attention". So of course, all the ladies at the table got a kick out of her comment and we laughed a good minute about it. My response was, "Well, let me think about it". Because I have a passion for producing and hosting events, it didn't take long for my creative flow to kick in. I started immediately giving some serious thought about what a class of that magnitude would actually look like. As most who know me should know…. I titled the class before midnight and started a plan.

The title that I fell in love with was "Mastering the Art of Flirting". But it didn't give me a complete fulfillment. I knew that there was no way that I would be lecturing or teaching a session on how to flirt! Instead, I wanted to share with that the real purpose for the class was actually to show ladies that it takes MORE than just flirting to capture the attention of **anyone**. A person has to be completely confident in who they are and in their own personal purpose in life. This is when I immediately said to myself "Flirting is more than just being cute, or having a pretty smile"....Then Voila! I knew that the title of the session would change to ***"Mastering the art of flirting; More Than Just A Pretty Smile" [Presented by Kelly Ragin]***. I booked a small conference room at a very nice hotel in Buckhead, Atlanta, had flyers designed, initiated my Eventbrite page for ticketing and started advertising the next day! I was READY!! Well, at least I thought I was ready.

I had about 15 women to register. The conference room held a capacity of 50 people. In my "not ready" mind, I didn't think 15 people was ample enough. As I approached the date, I made a decision to cancel. That was a move made by a woman (me) who was not confident in her ability to reach just ONE.

Later, after I canceled, I had so many people call to inquire about why the class had been canceled. I felt horrible and embarrassed. That moment was a major wake up call for me. I promised myself that going forward, I would never underestimate my ability to do what God has already equipped me to do. I would also never base my purpose on the number of people in the room. As my good sister friend Debra reminds me of often, "whomever is supposed to be in the room, will be in the room"!

Almost 2 years later, I partnered with my dear friend Mr. Perry Whaley (Founder and CEO of Vitiligo Man of Action (VMOA) in hosting our first Women's Empowerment Brunch. You guessed it! It was titled, "More Than Just A Pretty Smile". I had asked God to grant me another opportunity to do what I knew I was purposed to do. I promised that I would not squander that opportunity ever again. And so far, I'm holding my end of the promise. And we already know that God ALWAYS keeps His promise, even when we don't.

The Diagnosis

During the time period in August, 2018 --the week leading up to the Women's Empowerment brunch was crazy busy and somewhat stressful. I was working my full-time job, plus tying to finish up the final touches for the brunch. I had been noticing a blurriness in my left eye. Like many busy women, I noticed it but kept going. Kept moving and kept IGNORING a very important sign that indicated that something was wrong.

It was not until after the brunch that I would actually sit still long enough to recognize that the blurriness in my eye wasn't going away. I actually could not see!! So, that Sunday I became a wise woman, and went to urgent care for an evaluation.

Glad I went—but was very sad from the news I received. After various test over the next 2 to 3 days, including 3 vision tests, lab work and a spinal tap, I was diagnosed with **Multiple Sclerosis (MS)**. Vision loss is a symptom and a result of the onset of MS. This was a shocker for me and I certainly filled my bucket of tears. But after wiping my eyes dry, I then started on my game plan. Game plan? Yep! I wanted to get a handle on this new disease that was trying to set up shop in my body. First, I educated myself with my handy - dandy google friend. Learned the full definition of this monster of a disease and equipped myself so that I could answer questions from my immediate family. Trust me… I struggled to tell my family…. especially my daughters, but they truly showed up for me. I recalled the years of pouring into them the Word of God, and being consistent with them each morning with prayer and scriptures. It payed off!! Those two young women of mine came to my room one evening, and they both prayed over me while I was in bed. Whew!! Things were never the same after that. I felt proud that they knew that power of prayer and that prayer certainly does change things. I also knew that my healing was on the way!

After the diagnosis and receiving treatment, it took about 4 months before my vision was restored.

I can truly say that I understand the importance of …

"Walking by Faith and Not by sight"

Perseverance

How do you move forward when you feel that everything is spinning around you? This is how I had been feeling for the past 3 years. I could never put my finger on what was going on with me internally, mentally or physically. After my diagnosis, it all started to come together. Certain ailments made more sense, and the multiple "brain fogs" definitely made sense too. Due to MS, I've experienced a lot that caused anguish and anxiety. But through it all I learned PERSEVERANCE.

Perseverance. The ability to hang in there when you feel like giving up. That's my definition. Sometimes we don't see the happy ending. There are also times when you are in the thick of it, doubt creeps in and sets up shop. I remember during the time when I had lost my vision being very depressed. I could only think about the "what ifs". What if I can never see again out of my left eye? What if it shows up in the other eye? (and it actually did a few months later). What if I can never drive again? What if something worse happens after this? These were just a few questions that I battled with for a good little while. It was NOT easy. But I decided that I had to deal with the reality of my situation. I wanted to question God but I also knew that was useless because he orchestrates our lives with a Purpose. So in knowing all of this, I surrendered my pain. All of it. I started talking to myself daily. And it helped. I encouraged myself. Then over time, I would play music that inspired me. I absolutely love music. All kinds of music; but gospel is my first love. So, it didn't take long after getting my praise-on that I would find the joy that never left me.

See sometimes, it's just easier to blame God than to take some self-reflection. When you take a loooooooong good look at yourself, you may see some things you didn't notice before. Things that need to change. Things that need to be removed. Especially toxins. We take in toxins every day. Through bad food, beverages, chemicals, AND PEOPLE. Detoxing is mandatory if you desire to live a life with purpose.

I attended a virtual conference hosted by my business coach, Becky A. Davis, founder of BOSSPRENEUR Business Circle. One of her guests was none other than, Ms. Mikki Taylor, The Editor-at-Large for Essence Magazine. Ms. Taylor left us with some powerful tools to use when in situations that will require perseverance. In my own words, here's what I heard:

1. Make self-care a priority. It's indeed necessary. We must do the internal work. Inspect yourself! Exercise. It's an excellent stress reliever. Drink water. Hydrate, hydrate, hydrate! Release clutter. At home and in your head.

2. Guard your vision space. Protect your mental. We have the authority over what holds us down. We also have the authority to change our voice. We get to decide.

3. Build your spiritual muscle. This is the most important one for me. If we don't have a connection to the Most High…nothing we do will matter.

4. Be a Change Agent. Keep an Open mind.

5. Ask yourself "what can I accomplish today?" …then do it!

6. Tap into your inner celebration circle. It's important to keep people around you who affirm and who also checks you! Do you know who should be in our circle? Do an assessment.

7. Step out of your comfort zone! We don't have time to be lonely or bored!

"Spiritual preparation meets itself for what's ahead"
-Mikki Taylor

How did I regain my smile?

So, yes. I'm indeed more than just a pretty smile. But there were times where I lost my smile. How did I regain my smile? Here are a few real-life action steps that whipped me back into shape:

- Stay positive

It's so easy to let the negativity creep in. This is why it's vital that we guard our entire being. Put the stop sign at the door! Surround yourself with positive thinking, speaking, moving people. And quickly dismiss the ones who are not.

- Be kind…. to everyone

I truly believe that scripture that says, "Do unto others as you would have done unto you". It really is just as simple as that.

- Keep your promise

Do what you said you were going to do. It builds your integrity and your character.

- Be Grateful. Seriously.

A lesson I learned is that when you show gratitude for your blessings. …big or small, they multiply. It's the same as being a cheerful giver. Do it with a SMILE! If you lost your smile….I assure you that after becoming a "giver", your smile will re-appear!

- Dance

Oh how sweet it is! Dancing is a stress reliever and also makes you forget about the blues in that moment.

- Dream Big. Then pursue it. Imagine where you'll land!

Please don't ever stop dreaming. PLEASE. As a little

girl, my mother had wall art all around my bedroom. I grew up seeing the words:

DREAM- BELIEVE and ACHIEVE. I never knew how important these 3 words would become in my life. It's just amazing to me how relevant they are to my existence. Dream as big as you want, but don't just leave it there. Put in the work. Go after what you want. If God brought the thought to you, that simply means He can also manifest it for you.

The Lotus Flower...
Grows in Muddy Waters

Have you ever seen a lotus flower? It's one of the most beautiful flowers ever! It has such an intricate architectural growth design. God is so amazing to me. Out of ALL of the beauty in this world, none of it could ever be duplicated exactly how God made it.

This is how I view the lotus flower. The definition of the Lotus flower states that it is regarded in many different cultures, especially in eastern religions, as a symbol of purity, enlightenment, self-regeneration and rebirth. Its characteristics are a perfect analogy for the human condition; **even when its roots are in the dirtiest waters, the Lotus produces the most beautiful flower**.

I make note about the Lotus flower because its symbolic meaning was recently introduced to me. I wanted to know more about it and why this flower was chosen as the designated symbol for this particular interest group.

Well, after reading the excerpt on it, I now know exactly why. I love that it still grows into this beautiful, exotic yet pure exquisite flower.

God is showing us that he can change anything into something wonderful. Please remember that no matter what your situation looks like, or how dim the lights are, or how muddy the waters are in which you stand….God still has His hands on you. Run the race. Complete the course. Stand Tall and BLOOM! I love the quote that says, "Bloom where you are planted!". Don't allow the whispers and stares to hold you back. BLOOM, I SAY… BLOOM!!

The "Queen Bee"

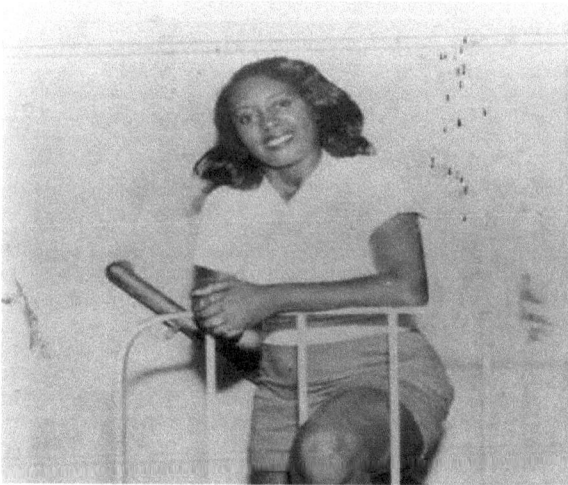

A dedication to my mother and maternal grandmother.

When I think of my grandmother, I think of the term, "queen bee". She was truly **"More than Just a Pretty Smile"**! For me, that is who she is and who she will always "bee". Vera Bell Nix. Born with grace and beauty! My family is quite fortunate. May, 2010 will mark the year and time when this magnificently blessed woman transitioned to paradise. The queen graced us with many years of her beautiful presence. I pray we can all have long-life and make our mark in the universe as she has done for us.

In writing this article, it gave me great pleasure in reminiscing over my childhood years. Grandmama, as I affectionately call her, did NOT play! So many things come to mind when I reflect. Things like, knowing "she'd better only call your name once", or "make sure you don't let that door slam", or "don't come back in here until the sun has gone down!" Those were the younger years; a place where I am sure many could relate to those "commandments". However, I am so grateful to have had the guidance of a true lady. We do not see that often these days. As I grew older, my grandmother became a tremendously strong influence in my life. I take nothing away from my mother, because as the saying goes, "Fruit doesn't fall far from the tree". There is nothing like a mother's love….and when you add and stir in Grandma's love—it makes for an even sweeter recipe. I do not think I have enough space to write about my affection for our "sweetie pie".

Question of the millennium…. where have the real women gone? I am still baffled, even today, at the generation that serves us presently. This of course, does not belittle all of the women in the world…for I AM WOMAN too! I only wish (how I wish!) there was a log or journal from back in the day on How to be a lady 101, or How to be a Mama 102. Have you ever taken notice to a woman who walks in the room and commands attention or respect by her mere presence? Can this prestigious way of life be taught or learned? Wishful thinking? Well, one thing I know for sure…. that's Mama Vera! Such elegance in her walk. Such sophistication in her dress. So much pizzazz, yet wisdom in her talk….and an overwhelming abundance of confidence in her beautiful, mahogany, ever-glowing brown countenance.

I listened countless times to Grandma's wisdom. I may have heard the same stories 3 times a week. However, it is not because she was forgetful. I had to learn that it was because the stories have relevance. Mama Vera was one of the strongest women I know. At the age of 11, she became motherless. Her mother died of tuberculosis. She then, was raised by her grandmother, Moriah Haynes (the other queen). As an adult, she married and gave birth to five children (today, I would be put in an asylum if I had more than two). Then, women knew how to be mothers. Good mothers. Many, many years have since passed and she is STILL an awesome mother! Constantly wanting the best for her family. A-L-L of her family. I have watched her care tirelessly for two daughters on their dying beds of cancer. The horrible disease that plagues so many today. She cared for them as if they were babies. A true mother. She was there until the end. I witnessed her share beautiful moments of happiness during joyous occasions in our family from weddings to birthday celebrations. She could clean out a freezer (mine and yours) to pack meals for wayward family members. Each time, I would think, "this lady doesn't miss a beat". Most importantly, I gained much admiration for her in seeing her live a true Christian lifestyle. Her love for God supersedes it all. She was our teacher for a lot of lessons learned. One of the most valuable messages she gives and continues to give is "Baby…..a peace of mind is better than anything, any day". I live by these words TODAY. Grandma went through a lot in her life. Too much actually, for such a queen as she…. but her love for God, her family and self were all the example I've ever needed to know what it takes to be the next……. Queen Bee.

P.S.: Did I forget to tell you that she eloped at the age of 70? All hail to the queen! I truly miss her….

Three Proud Generations of Wonderful Ladies
From Left to right, Mother, Mrs. Linda L. Stepp, Grandmother, Mrs. Vera Brown and Granddaughter, Ms. Kelly Ragin

Believe

BELIEVE. This is one of my favorite words.
Throughout my home, you are bound to see it in almost
every room in some shape, fashion or form. Why is it
that this particular word is so powerful? Ever since I was
a little girl, this word has dangled in my face. I recall
my mother purchasing wall art for my bedroom, in the
form of words. She placed these words on my wall, just
above my bed. The words that I vividly remember…
some 40 years later are, DREAM, BELIEVE,
ACHIEVE. Now as a 7-year-old, I had no real concept
to what the true definition was for each of those words.
Today, the term is called AFFIRMATIONS.

See, I strongly believe that we should AFFIRM ourselves
daily. By this I mean, speak life into your own lives.
FIRST. Belief first starts with a thought. Then it moves
into, perhaps, a dream or desire for something powerful
in your life. Or even something simple.   Then of course,
finally, it's now up to you to decide if you actually
believe in that vision, or dream whatever it is. Do you?

I would easily say that, Believing is the same as having
FAITH. And we've heard the scripture a gazillion times
that states "Now Faith, is the Substance of things hoped

for, and the evidence of things unseen". Hebrews 11: 1. I also love the quote:

"Putting Feet to your Faith".

Putting feet to your faith basically means, DO SOMETHING WHILE YOU WAIT ON GOD! He's God, and doesn't need our help. But I believe He wants to see if we are going to be diligent in working for Him, while we wait. Also, what are you doing towards the preparation or development for your dream? Heard the term, "whistle while you work? "Well, all this means is…. Keep a positive attitude while working towards your goal. At least, that's my interpretation.

What are you believing God for today? I would like to encourage you to first, DREAM BIG. Mama constantly reminds me, "Child, ain't nothing too hard for God". So, I often find myself telling myself these very words. See sometimes, we want things to happen, WHEN we want them to happen. Oh, my goodness! Don't we know that God holds the blueprints? I love to encourage my family and friends to create Vision Boards. I have one of my own. And YES!! It works!! Now, you and I both know that cutting up pictures from magazines and using our lil' glue sticks to paste them on a board, is NOT gonna do the trick, like a Jeannie in the bottle. WE KNOW THIS! But what it does, is, it forces us to face our dreams DAILY. AFFIRM our BELIEF. And garner patience, as God does what HE does best. PROVIDES.

DREAM BIG. God's doors are HUGE!

Women and WHY WE ROCK, GRIND, SLAY, & Pray.

ROCK STEADY BABY!

It's such an honor to give homage to ALL WOMEN in recognition of International Women's Month during the month of March.

Hey ladieeees….
We Rock, Grind, Slay and definitely …we PRAY!

In this God-given role as Wo-Man, I've found life to be quite interesting. And quite challenging too at times. However, one thing I've learned about me as a woman, is that I'm especially resilient. Something you don't find out, until you're forced to…find out! As I reflect over my life, I've pretty much, darn near mastered resilience. Funny thing is, it feels like I was wired all along to bounce back anyway. It was nothing I read, or instructed to do. I just did.

The overall blessing is, being present to have seen and witnessed so many other women overcome some of the worst challenges in their lives. From my beautiful grandmothers, to my Mother, Aunts, family, friends and co-workers and even strangers on those TV talk shows.

I'm certainly a witness myself. I've **endured** marital abuse, being used, financial drain, being neglected, judgement, work-place exhaustion, parental woes, health challenges, and spiritual warfare.

And still **I RISE**. And so, can YOU!! I GRIND   FOR MINE!

All I have ever known is watching the women in my family grind. HARD! Whether it was working a 9 to 5, or having 2 or sometimes 3 jobs. That in itself has shown me a couple of things.

1) The importance of working hard for what you need and desire. 2) and…. that clearly, there were not enough good men around to help them!

All jokes aside. Back in the day, women were taught to rely on their men to help them financially. While there was absolutely nothing wrong with that formula. I'm an old school soul myself, so who knows how I would have perceived that type of upbringing during those times. However, today things are vastly different for women in this era.

Women are grinding harder because quite frankly; there's no other choice. We do what "we have to do, until we don't have to". Then there's that issue of women [mainly African American women] having the better paying jobs versus their spouses or partners. Be that as it may, we put in the work. This doesn't mean that the brothers are not working hard. It only means that women are simply continuing their grind as their grandmothers and mothers have done. Feeding our children and paying the bills is what we do best. By any means necessary. Get it Gurrrrls!!

On my day job before retirement, I served the public as a Federal Employee. I loved my job and was gainfully employed [by the grace of God] for close to 30 years. Then suddenly, we had a Government shutdown. Oh Lord!!!! "What in the world am I gonna do if they don't pay us??" This was my first thought. My wheels started turning……and fast! I began to tap into my resources. Sure, I had a few pennies saved, but if I used it ALL to cover the time frame of being out of work, then what? Talkin' bout a sistah being stressed! But one thing for certain; I knew God would provide. I also knew that I had enough skills and talents to always get a J-O-B. Fortunately, the Government shutdown only lasted 3 weeks. **I was gratefu**l. However, it sure was enough to put a fire under my feet! I promised myself, never again would I not be prepared.

Immediately, after that time, I started on my side hustles. I started a travel business, launched an Empowerment organization, Events Business, partnered and became co-owner of a fitness studio, coaching, and started working on one of my passions....my beloved freelance writing. No matter whether you start something brand new or tap into something you do well, the key is to keep it moving!

In the course of working your side hustle, you may find that there's no real interest as you had hoped. It's O-K!! You tried. Put it in file drawer #8. Why 8? The number 8 is a continual loop. There's no real end to it. Years ago, I opened a Home Day Care. Had been on my "Good Government Job" for 10 years at that time. Scared to pieces to leave my job. But I wanted to be home with youngest daughter, Erin who was only a few months old. I only have 2 children. At that time, my oldest daughter, Ericka was 4 years old. I wanted to be more available for her too. The business went very well. Actually, extremely well. But I later realized that I was not cut out for "staying home".

Eventually, I found my way back to the office. With no regrets. One reason is, I learned that I COULD DO IT! I opened my first real business on my own. I was so proud of myself. Another thing I gained, was a new skill. I also gained a new motto. Which is, to NEVER SAY NEVER. See, even though I preferred to be in the office environment, I would never allow myself to say,

"I will never do Home Day Care ever again." Nope! Won't come from me. Simply because, I now have a skill that no one can take from me in the event that I need to make money in times of a crisis. I will always be on my grind; as long as God gives me strength.

SHE SLAYS! Yes, she does! - Werk it girl! - She Did THAT! – OH NO SHE DIDN'T! - Yes, Hun-TY! Slay Gurl, Slay! - I SEE YOU GIRL! – DO IT GIRLFRIEND! – YOU GO GIRL!

These are just a few slang phrases that you may hear from time to time in reference to a sophisticated, classy, got-it-going-on, sistah passing by your way. And more than likely it's going to come from another Sistah. I've often heard that women usually dress to impress other women, not so much as men. This is probably true in most cases. We as women will be the first to notice what another woman is wearing before a man does. Men may notice how a lady looks in a pair of jeans. Whereas, a woman, may recognize what type or brand of jeans she's wearing first. We are truly, peculiar creatures.

Thing is, I've learned to wear what works for me. I've learned to be authentically-ME. Took a while to get here. But I'm here and there's no turning back! If you prefer to prance in your 6-inch heels daily (like my baby girl, bless her heart), then do it. However, if you are a "sneaker head" … (much like my oldest daughter), then do that too!

Ladies, let's work on being more in Love with ourselves.

Our inner selves more so, than making "slaying" materialistically, our priority. We truly slay in so many other ways. But when you feel GREAT about who you are, it shows on the outside too. Confidence becomes the glow that glistens on your face when you OWN IT. And believe it or not, others see it too.

So, go on! *SLAY, ALL DAY!*

SHE PRAYS!

Prayer is the key to being Wo-man. Period. In our vital role as woman, we are so many other things. We're wives, mothers, daughters, sisters, girlfriends, Secretaries, homemakers, cooks, nurses, and oh my goodness… she-ro's in all things!

In order to make it through the day, prayer is essential. Starting your day in prayer or meditation gives you the jumpstart needed to face the unknown beyond the doors of the peace of your home. I love seeing the manifestation of what a consistent prayer life brings to the weary relentless soul. Prayer changes things! Indeed, it does. In Thessalonians 5;17, we are urged to **Pray without ceasing.** Let's continue to go to God's throne about those very things that plague our hearts. God is listening. And more importantly, HE ANSWERS!

That broken thing you keep trying to put back together can't even compare with that beautiful thing that's waiting to be built.

Relationships and Your Well-Being

Do relationships affect our health and wellbeing?

The answer to this one… EMPHATICALLY—Y.E.S! ABSOLUTELY!

In a nutshell, relationships can either make you, or break you. But no matter the feat…it's up to you just how much energy you give and how much you allow it to affect your wellbeing.

Relationships come in many forms. In this forum, we're going to discuss Man/Woman, Boy/Girl relationships.

When we fall in love, or in DEEP LIKE, studies have shown that the "Being in Love" Feeling helps boost endorphins, and can truly be a good cure for; or close to it.

It's also an EXCELLENT chaser to depression. For many reasons, people fall into the slump of the "d" word (Depression). Usually, it is because of what the person feels he/she is missing. I recently read an article titled, "Hacking into your Happiness". The article was referencing toxins and the chemical chemistry that our bodies make naturally.

However, I would like to give an alternative perspective. Below is a list of reasons why people choose to commit or seek relationships. H-E-A-L-T-H-Y Relationships;

that is.

REASONS TO SEEK HEALTHY RELATIONSHIPS

1. Sense of belonging/Feeling Needed
I am a firm believer that, no matter what comes out of a person's mouth, everyone wants to feel needed. It's such a good feeling knowing that someone was desires what you have and own. Your very own personality! Once we love on ourselves, then Mr. or Mrs. "Right" will see that value through you.

2. Partnership
Back in my Girl Scout Leader days, during outings, I would ALWAYS tell my troop…

"OK! Buddy Up!". Simply meaning—find your buddy, connect, and do not leave her side for this entire trip. Well, I would venture to say that in committed relationships, if we "Buddied UP" -

We could weather quite a few storms. Partnership brings about togetherness and the sense that you have a reliable source, outside of yourself.

3. Security/Stability
Security. In addition, I'm not referring to the "Mall Cop". But referring to that old adage question of – So, what do you have to bring to the table? When couples are dating, this question comes up…but not always discussed. It's OK TO ASK! A friend and I have these discussions often. The consensus is that,

we've denounced the old saying of "just meet me in the middle". I prefer the saying… Just meet me at the starting line! Let's BOTH bring something worthy to the front line. AND FINISH STRONG!

4. Stress Reducer

I believe that we tend to worry less when we have a partner. After all, this means you have someone to share the load. You also have someone to whom you can vent or get FREE THERAPY!

5. Better Sexual health

SEX. Not a bad word. Definitely has its benefits when you have the right dance partner…. In many ways. But it can also give false pretense that it can be the cure for true happiness. Yes—it gives happy feelings but we just need to be sure that we are being responsible with our actions and those happy feelings.

6. HEALTHY Mental Health

I know that reads strangely, but having HEALTHY mental health is vital. So often we run from seeking help, counsel or therapy when it comes to our inside brain. There's absolutely nothing to be ashamed of considering that we didn't create ourselves. Now when it comes down to merging your life with someone who's not mentally well this could be problematic or even a matter of life and death. Mental health disorders can create all kinds of toxicity in your life, In your family and in your home. SEEK HELP IMMEDIATELY if you are the person suffering from the disorders, or if your gut is telling you it's your partner. Both lives matter.

7. Spiritual connection

Finally, having a cool connection is nice –but there is NOTHING like connecting spiritually. Sharing Faith in a higher source, outside of yourselves is vital. Starting your day together in prayer is especially special---as well as always having your own private prayer time. I have a quote for my home that I refer to regularly.

"OUR Faith in OUR GOD, are the wings, to OUR Love". (Kr)

When Passion Meets Purpose

In this phase of my life, I have vowed to do whatever it takes to achieve optimal health for myself. I have more dreams and goals to obtain, and don't want any ailments or disabilities to block them. I had always looked forward to being a grandmother, and my constant prayer is asking God for "Long Life and Good Health!" so that I could see that day. Now that my handsome grandson Jayce has graced us with his presence, I want to do everything I need to do to stay well and healthy so that I can bond with him; and watch him successfully grow into the man that God created him to be in this world.

In 2014, I went to the doctor for a wellness check concerning pain that just would not go away. When I think about my doctor's visit, I giggle to myself because I think about my maternal grandmother. Her view regarding her personal health was truly not a laughing matter. Grandma did not play when it came to taking care of herself, Ms. Vera. The family also joked and said, if her pinky toe was hurting, she was on her way to the emergency room. Well, we joked about it, but the truth of the matter is, we, as women, don't seem to take time out to see about ourselves as often as we should. We are too busy taking care of everyone else.

Well, I must admit, I'm glad that my grandmother showed us an example on how to love and take care of ourselves. So, my visit to the doctor turned out to be a life-saving visit. Turns out, I had a congenital condition that resulted in the growth of a tumor that could have easily grown aggressively--- fast into Abdominal cancer. According to my specialist, there was nothing that could have been done to prevent it. However, there are tons that can be done to obtain and retain optimal health. Here are a few tips that the Office on Women's Health advise:

STEPS FOR BETTER HEALTH: Over Age 40. (www.womenshealth.gov)

[The website actually breaks down the different age categories starting at age 20 – 90]

- Get an annual well-woman visit.
- Get my blood pressure checked
- Eat healthy
- Maintain a healthy weight
- Get at least 30 minutes of physical activity
- Quit smoking
- Limit Alcohol Use
- Talk to doctor about domestic violence

Sometimes it takes a tragedy, or a major life event to shake us into "getting it right". I prayed and asked God to give me a plan for getting it right. On the ride home one evening, my prayers were answered. I found a newly opened, Personal Group Fitness Training studio in my community, literally 5 minutes from home. It was called ICANFITNESS-ATLANTA. I eagerly inquired about the details, and then suddenly, I found myself now doing squats, laps, and crunches –just to name a few activities that I also teasingly refer to as torture, but the good kind.

Often times, women over the age of 40 have a more challenging time when it comes to losing weight or getting fit. It's not nearly as easy as it looks in those Commercials.

After leaving my post-surgery doctor's appointment, I vividly remember my doctor's words; "I NEED YOU TO LOSE AT LEAST 30 – 40 POUNDS". This was a definite SWIFT KICK IN THE ASS! One that made me realize that I had work to do. Today, I'm still working towards that goal. I will also be the first to tell you that getting fit is not for wimps! But it is so worth it. As it turns out, my consistency in attending the fit training classes, led to something just as beneficial. A great business opportunity.

I'm a firm believer that when you are positioned where you are supposed to be, then what's for you, will come to you. Through several discussions and collaborating with my then personal trainer, Mr. Brian Meadows, and Owner of ICANFITNESS-ATLANTA (now called Smart Fit, By Brian), we shook hands December 2015 and I became Co-owner. It was the one pursuit I asked God for in achieving her optimal health. I didn't take the opportunity for granted and I recognize that God's hands have never left my presence.

Being co-owner of a fitness studio taught me a great deal. It was an unexpected opportunity, but the timing was excellent because I learned about partnership. This was 5 years ago. I asked to be bought out of the company because I also later learned the importance of staying in your lane (I'm truly laughing out loud while writing this sentence). I have zero regrets. Many lessons learned. Friendships gained, and I became a more focused woman.

During that time, I posted a Facebook message to my friends. I reminded them of this:

> "No. I'm not a size 2. 10. or 12. But I do represent the Average size woman. No excuse though to NOT exercise. I'm a work in progress. I've fallen off the wagon a few times…and sometimes just stare at it for a minute. Lol. But I'm determined to live a HEALTHY lifestyle. Ladies over 40…we know it's NOT easy…but we gotta do it. Let's support each other. Whether you check us out at ICANFITNESS-Atlanta or not…WORK ON YOU! You're worth it. We have beautiful lives to live. So. Let's live. Longer. I CAN. YOU CAN. WE CAN."

During that time, the fitness studio had become a place of refuge for a lot of people in my community. A sense of purpose, and everyone pretty much has the same or similar goals which is the desire to reach their optimal health". You must take a stance within yourself and be in it, to win it! And by that, I mean YOU! —as the winner.

When I share this part of my story with folks, I'm always quick to say, "Please don't look for that size 2 chic". I remind them that business is business. However, it is certainly my goal to one day grace the Before and After pics at some point in my life. Meanwhile, I will continue striving and dancing. Anything to get the body moving!

Outside of getting the physical body in order, everyone knows that it's just as important to get your mind and soul in order as well. This is where Passion meets Purpose and Women's Health marries Empowerment. In 2008, I Founded an organization called KellyKares-Empowering Events. My founding scripture is:

Proverbs 17:17 A Friend Loves At All Times

KellyKares is an organization to promote and foster empowering events that serve a higher purpose. It also provides a continuous avenue for women (and all people) to share their stories of challenge and triumph. I have such a passion for my true calling which is simply, bringing people together. My love of family, friends, love and life has truly been exemplary –I pray -in the events I produce. One of my favored events recently has been the hosting of "Vision & Purpose Board Parties" and "The Battle of the Sexes". Both bring an evening of food, fun, music, laughter and Good Times…but with PURPOSE.   I've also had a love for journaling and writing since I was a teen. I feel so fortunate to have been given the creativity to produce platforms that allow others to share their stories of challenge and triumph. In addition to KellyKares, I founded MyStory Publications. This company produces digital and print magazines, book collaboration projects and blog articles and so much more.   And finally, I would say that God has a sense of humor and used my gift of gab. I'm proud to also now be a certified Relationships and Lifestyles Coach. This role also gives me an opportunity to do group coaching and empowerment speaking. I simply have a love for people, and seeing people in my community succeed.

In the progression of merging my passions into purpose, God allowed me to gain new skills, new partnerships and new collaborations. The reason this story is important to me is because I truly gained a clearer vision for my life's purpose. It's more than just a title, or making a cute name for myself or business. For me, it's more about making a difference in the lives of my community.

Perfect Peace

Watching someone experience the loss of 2 loved ones
(a husband AND wife) 1 week apart from the other was
definitely enough to make me SIT DOWN. BUT as
with most deaths...it forces you to think about your own
life and hereafter. Am I living right? Is my living in vain?
What's my purpose? All that, and then some.

Driving into work one morning, listening to the radio, I
heard a minister's message. It was on PEACE. NOW....
generally, I flip through stations looking for something
"peaceful"...musically for my morning commute.
However, this message caught my ear.

In a nutshell, he reminded us that PEACE was a gift
from God. You can't buy it, nor can u create it on your
own. We ALL want peace. God is the MASTER builder
of this PERFECT gift.

Well, after receiving THAT dreaded call that we knew
ultimately was coming (due to terminal cancer of
relative) that morning I was saddened...but her daughter
immediately followed and said..."I'm sad too...but she
had this "PERFECT PEACE" on her face. Those were
just the exact words I needed to hear! To be reminded
of...

God is our REWARDER....to those who faithfully and diligently seek HIM. We ALL have different journeys in "this" life. But the same bridge to cross in the end.

DO YOU WANT PERFECT PEACE? Remember....
it's God's gift to all who put their mind on Him. God's word says boldly that
"I will give you Perfect peace, whose mind is stayed on me".
Even in the midst of YOUR storm, or heartache, bereavement, AND LONELINESS... YOU CAN HAVE......"PERFECT PEACE".

Kelly Y. Ragin
Biography

Mrs. Kelly Ragin is a woman of God first., Mother of 2 exceptional young adult daughters. Founder of *KellyKares*, an organization that promotes events that serve a higher purpose for Empowerment through several avenues.

Kelly is also the Founder, Publisher and Editorial Director, for **MyStory** Magazine Publications where she provides a magazine media venue to share stories from wedding announcements, to Triumphant and Overcomer's stories, and other personal stories of Business Success. Her hope is to open varied avenues for the community to share their stories. Her tagline for the publication is MyStory Publications; **"WE ALL HAVE ONE"**.

A proud native Atlantan. Born and raised in Decatur, Georgia… who doesn't mind being called the rhetorical "Grady Baby"! A graduate of Towers High School, attended Georgia State University, Majored in Nursing. Kelly started her federal career in 1988 with the Health Care Financing Administration, Division of Medicare as a Work-study student. Later, moved on to the Centers for Disease Control and Prevention (CDC).

For almost 30 years Kelly spent her 9 to 5 as a Public Health Servant; and her last position as a Public Health Analys with the CDC in Atlanta, GA. She does not take her journey for granted one bit. In her last role before retirement in 2019, she worked in the Office of the Chief of Staff, supporting the CDC Director as a liaison to the public and the various centers and programs throughout the CDC agency; concerning issues related to the Nation's Public Health matters.

Some of Kelly's affiliations are: Bosspreneur Business Circle (BBC), Atlanta Spotlight on Business/Xperience Connections and Business group, Dualpreneur Group, CDC's Association for Professional Women (APW), CDC's Local Chapter of The Blacks in Government (BIG), Girl Scouts (she served as a leader and coordinator for 10 years- A very rewarding service oriented role she loved!). And since age 13, a very, proud member of the Beulah Missionary Baptist Church, in Decatur, GA under the leadership of Rev. Jerry D. Black.

In 2014, Kelly was honored as a BLACK WOMEN ROCK recipient through, the CDC chapter of Blacks in Government. She also was awarded the Trail Blazer award in 2016. Kelly previously served as Board Member, on the Board of Directors for her community and has partnered with other non-profit organizations to serve where needed. Kelly is also a certified Relationships and Lifestyles Coach and Certified Freelance writer. She has served as a part time writer for DESIRE HEALTH Magazine, Inc. based in San Bernardino, CA. She's also an aspiring author with an eagerness to share her testimonies of challenge and triumph. Currently penning her first autobiography/memoir titled:

"Restored Wings" and a novella titled: "Crossing the Line", along with several other book projects. She has written numerous impactful articles that can be found on both websites.

Finally, Kelly credits her mother, Ms. Linda Stepp, for being her "she-ro" in all things. Learning about business, professionalism, and work ethics came easy because Mom was an excellent teacher. However, it was Mom's "living example" that taught Kelly how to be a REAL and TRUE friend to the world. She saw behind closed doors a real woman of God whose integrity spoke volumes in her walk and in her talk. Eternally grateful for Mama.

Passions & Hobbies: Writing/journaling, music (Gospel, Contemporary jazz & old school R &B), reading, traveling, and antique/thrift consignment shopping, cooking for her sister-friends & family. An entrepreneur at heart, she often likes to ask…" So, …what's your passion? Kelly is the author of 3 published books and several empowerment articles. She loves empowering the person whose gifts are shining through, but sitting stagnant. Also, a certified relationships coach, she offers group coaching to women through speaking opportunities to uplift those who have struggled with issues in their marriages or partner relationships. Kelly is also known as the Lovepreneur and says "I didn't go through all that for nothin'!"

DEDICATION

God has a way of allowing people's paths to cross at a particular time for his purpose. I thought that it would be fitting to express my deepest appreciation for you and for our friendship. Thank you for supporting me from day one of this project. You always encourage and push me to let the world see my gifts and you remind me that becoming a better "me" will serve as the roadmap to help build better generations. You always saw my worth, even when I couldn't see it in myself. Your vision helped me to see my own value and the true essence of my being. Your friendship has shown me such an unwavering and selfless love. You're always in my corner and have my back in whatever God places to do in my heart. To you again, I just want to say: Thank You.

The Effects of a Father

"Fathers are the 'measuring stick."

It is my belief that some of the emotional and physical ills of our society can be traced back to the absence of our biological fathers. Whether physically or emotionally, there is something unique about his role in the life of a child.

Fathers have the ability to influence their daughter's lives either positively or negatively, as they are our first introduction to what masculinity looks like. They are huge role models in how we develop in life and set the standard for our relationships with men. Fathers are the "measuring stick", as I call it, by which their daughter's will judge other men, romantically or as friends.

Early on, we learn what to look for in a future partner by observing our father's character and behaviors, making it easier for us in choosing a mate. A father influences how his daughter feels about herself; he not only brings out her best qualities, but he compliments her physical beauty as well. She is less likely to be dependent on man's validation, simply because she's already been celebrated and showered with unconditional love from her father. His love, encouragement and support are critical for her development into womanhood. He gives her a sense of identity that provides her confidence to make better choices in life.

So, what happens when what you think your father *should* be, doesn't line up to the father that you grew up with? Do you know what kind of affect that can have on your life? Well, let me tell you my story.

The attack on my life has always been against my self-esteem and my self-worth. It started early in my childhood, when my father would say negative things about me that formed insecurities that I still wrestle with. These early childhood experiences subconsciously shaped who I became and influenced my choices and mindset.

I grew up in a house where my mother made most of the decisions, while my father passively followed her lead. Although my father was present physically, he rarely participated in my life. I contribute some of that to the role that men played 'back in the day', where fathers were providers, while mothers took care of the home and nurtured the children. I believe that his mindset was based on what he saw as a child, or the idea that fathers were only responsible for working and earning money for the family. This taught me to be mindful of my experiences, because we grow up and treat our children the way we were treated.

My father never talked much about his upbringing, but I later found out about issues he faced with instability growing up that followed him into his adult life. I realized that a healthy and stable home environment was important for a child's emotional development. Although some change in a child's life is normal and anticipated, sudden and dramatic disruptions can be extremely stressful and affect children's overall sense of security.

Unfortunately, a lot of homes experience disruption in one area that triggers disruption in other areas, resulting in a series of events that can compound over time. Over time, I had to forgive my father knowing that he did the best he could with what he knew. Although I never disrespected my father, I didn't view him as much of a leader in our home or look up to him like most daughters do. At that point, I began to search outside of home for what I didn't get from my father which led me to look for love in all of the wrong places. At the end of the day, I just needed my Dad. I needed that role model to give me direction in my life. I needed the validation and assurance from my father to know that there is nothing that I could ever do that would keep him from loving me. I needed to know that he would be there for me, simply because I was his. The little girl in me always wanted to make my Dad proud and put a smile on his face, but over time, I discovered a love that changed my present reality.

When we think of the love of a father, who is a better example than our Heavenly Father? God has so many great things in store for us, however, many have a hard time trusting him because of how their own father has treated them. Sometimes we think that God's love is just like man's love when it is the complete opposite.

God is like none other and has an unconditional love that you can trust and depend on. When God looks at us, he doesn't see the flawed, messed-up person that we see in the mirror. Instead, he sees us in the finished state of who we are to be.

I couldn't comprehend just how much God really loved me because I never felt the unconditional love that I desired. I've only seen a love with conditions, not one based on acceptance of who I am. When I look back at my childhood, I began to see that my father caused me to view God the same way as I view man. I felt like to be approved by God, I needed to be perfect. I was always looking at my imperfections, shortcomings and weaknesses thinking that God would judge me because people did. But God loves me in spite of me. He knows everything that I have done, am doing and will do-- yet he still chose me.

A Letter to My Father

Dear Daddy,

I am writing this letter to forgive you for not being the father that I expected you to be. I have allowed what I didn't get from you to cause me to make decisions in my life that weren't the best for me because I didn't have you to show me who I was. I didn't have you to encourage me and to show me what a real man looked like and how I should be treated. So, it caused me to seek validation outside of myself and when I did, it left me feeling devalued and lacking love for myself. I realize that there are no perfect people, but I looked to you to give me something that you never received. I expected you to father me, without realizing that you may not have had a good example of one for yourself. Now, I realize that you did the best that you could with what you knew, and I will no longer hold any bitterness or unforgiveness against you.

Today, I am releasing all of the hurt and pain of my past that I have held against you for years and it will no longer keep me from reaching my full potential. I had to go through a lot to get to this point, but now, I recognize that I have worth. I am valuable and I am loved. Not because someone told me that I was, but because I finally realized it for myself. Because of this, I am now self-sufficient, strong and have dreams and vision for myself. Thank you, God, for bringing out the greatness in me that moments of crushing tried to destroy. Now, I am truly free to be me.

Sincerely,

Your daughter

When a Father is No Longer Around

"Be mindful of the decisions you make when disappointment hits."

In the midst of my journey to wholeness, I found myself maturing spiritually, but still had emotional voids. I was blessed to meet a pastor who changed my life in slow and subtle ways that I didn't expect. Over time, this divine connection became the example of a father that I needed.

While he was well-known around the world and influential in Atlanta, he was more than just a pastor-- he was like a father to me. Although I did not know him personally, I connected with him spiritually, and when he preached it was like he was all up in my Kool-Aid, *just* like a father. I loved, respected and honored him very much as I saw a lot of what I was looking for from my father in him. I can honestly say that he fathered me from a distance. He always nurtured and encouraged me, spoke life into me and told me who I was in God. He was the one God used to help give me my identity and build me up as a woman, who had been beaten down emotionally.

He loved and supported our congregation and prepared us physically, mentally, emotionally and spiritually for what we would face on this journey. It's only been three years since his death, and I've experienced some of the effects that happen when a child loses their father. Not only had I lost my biological father in 2012, but now I lost my spiritual father in 2017.

I know several "Daddy's Girls", who were so torn apart when their fathers died. You begin to wonder, "Who is going to be there for me now?", and, "Who is going to affirm me now?". Although I didn't recognize it at the time, I think I was a little mad with God for taking away such an influential person in my life. When you find something good that you've always wanted and then you lose it, it is absolutely heartbreaking.

So, during that time, I did what children do when they lose a parent…they rebel. I reverted back to looking for a man to affirm me in the absence of my biological and spiritual fathers. I learned that when tragedy hits, some of us scramble to find that place of comfort again and often times it can be going back to something or someone that isn't good for us. For me, my reaction to the disappointment took my life off-course. Word to the wise: *Be mindful of the decisions you make when disappointment hits.*

Finding Where I Fit In

"There was a lot of healing that had to be done and there's still much more."

Everyone is trying to find their place in life. We attach ourselves to certain groups just to have a sense of belonging because no one wants to feel like they are alone. I stumbled upon a series by Dr. Cindy Trimm called, "Discovering Where You Belong". It was not until I listened to this series, that I realized I had "Daddy Issues" that have affected my life more than I realized. I didn't know why I responded to certain things the way that I did until I identified with certain beliefs and attitudes that had become a part of my personality and controlled my life. When I talk about "Daddy issues", I am not just talking about the absence of a father or a poor relationship with your father, but how that state of fatherlessness frames you from your childhood.

People with "Daddy issues" approach life feeling like they don't have a safe and secure place in their father's heart. You don't get that sense of protection or belonging so you become self-centered and emotionally isolated. When this mentality is a part of your life, isolation and loneliness will cause you to seek comfort in other areas. You position yourself to gain the approval of others by seeking affirmations that say to you, "I am good enough to fit in".   These feelings can develop a stronghold in your mind.

The lack of his presence in my life both physically and emotionally reminded me of a lack of affirmation and acceptance. It made me feel unloved and unlovable, resulting in a negative approach in how I dealt with other relationships. It caused me to have distrust in relationships and friendships because I never felt secure enough that anyone really had my back. So, no matter how cool we were, I would keep my distance for fear of them rejecting me and leaving me even more damaged. It caused me to approach life with an independent, self-reliant attitude, not putting a lot of faith in people. So, if I couldn't do it, no one else was going to do it for me.

The only way that I found to change this mindset is to embrace and experience God's love. What do I have to lose? His love has got to be better than what I have experienced through man. You don't have to do anything to try and earn this love and you don't have to question his love. It is secure and comes from a place of pure acceptance. Eventually, you will learn to embrace God's love and acceptance through your identity in Christ that will ultimately bring your deliverance.

Parked at the Point of my Pain

"When you experience pain, you have to be very careful where you find relief."

You are the sum total of all of your choices. Where you are, whether good or bad is the result of your decisions. I once heard the saying: "Never make a permanent decision based off of a temporary situation". But so often, we do. Especially when we are in pain. When you experience pain, you have to be very careful where you find relief.

I allowed the pain of my disappointment and frustrations to not only cause me to make bad decisions, not choose satisfying my short-term pain over my eternal destiny. It kind of reminded me of the story of Esau and Jacob, when Esau gave up his birthright for the pot of stew. At the time, he valued the stew because he was more interested in filling his short -term desire than waiting on the long-term benefits of his inheritance.

Just like me, Esau wasn't able to see beyond the pain of the present moment. His birthright was way more valuable than a pot of stew, but the desire to fill his hunger caused him to lay down what was most valuable. Your choices will always be based on your values and how you choose will show what you prioritize the most. The breakdown between me and my father made me try and fill that void either with some*thing* or some*one*. I chose the latter.

At the point of my pain, I looked to someone who would value who I was and be a support to my calling as I supported theirs. In choosing to fill my void with a partner, I met someone and anticipated that things would eventually lead to marriage, but this was the very thing that God used to bring my brokenness to the surface.

In learning this new person, I found myself often upset with my expectations of him. I grew frustrated because I invested time into someone who I expected to invest time back into me. I was going through the motions, but inwardly I had shut down and built up walls. The bitterness, hurt and anger went on for years until I emotionally detached from the individual.

The situation showed me that I was looking for someone else to love and value me, when I should love and value myself FIRST. Although I was not wrong or unrealistic in what I was asking for, the problems come in when you demand someone to do for you what you should be doing for yourself. It is never anyone else's responsibility to make you feel good about yourself; that is something that must come from within.

Twisted Souls

During that same time, I began talking with a guy about the situation that I was in just to get some male guidance and insight into the psyche of a man. When we would talk, he would encourage and push me to be all that God was calling me to be. I would occasionally discuss more with him as time went on. He listened but never spoke bad about my situation but was always attentive to me and stressed the importance of me looking out for myself. I never realized that through our sharing and spending time together, we were developing a bond. The more I spent time with him and got to know him, he seemed to be a great friend to have in my life, but I was trying to figure out what I needed to do about this other relationship I was believing God to develop.

As years went on and things in the first situation were not going as I had anticipated, my focus shifted. By that time, I found myself having a connection with this new guy. I felt like it was cool since there was nothing physical going on, but our souls were so joined together that it felt like a developing relationship. Neither one of us had experienced such a strong connection like this but our hearts were open to one another and we couldn't seem to pull away. You have to be careful of the things you choose when you are hurting and experiencing disappointment.

Oftentimes, we make choices due to pain, disappointments and voids that we are trying to fill. I had always desired to be loved and treated the way he treated me, and that made it so much harder to pull away. The interesting part about the whole thing is that there was no sex involved. What we shared was deeper than our bodies; we shared our hearts and our dreams. I never thought that sharing those things would draw two people closer, but I was so wrong. I later realized that this is how intimacy evolves, through communication and spending time together.

Although I have never had an addiction, I can admit that for years, this friendship numbed the pain I had and fulfilled my deep desire to be loved. What I found out is that although we have a great relationship, it is not a relationship with another person that we need. It is a deeper relationship with God that helps us to heal and begin to love ourselves again.

I had to realize that sometimes people come into our lives to help expose things about us that need to be dealt with. They help us see things about ourselves. If you are single, everyone that comes into your life is not a potential spouse. They may have, like my friend did, come into your life to help you connect with the purpose and destiny that God has for you to help you become whole. At the end of the day, we chose to focus on what God called both of us to do. We must prioritize God's will over our own desires.

The Effects of Rejection

I never realized how deeply rejection affected me until I took a bold stance to face it head-on and not allow it to continue robbing me of my life. I believe that rejection had a lot to do with me not being able to connect to the true value of who I was. It's not just about facing rejection, but processing rejection in a healthy way when it happens to you. Rejection messes with your self-esteem and brings up all kinds of negative emotions. When people reject you like family, close friends and romantic relationships, it makes you feel that you are less than and unwanted. There are several emotions that come out of rejection that I experienced. There is the emotion called the "emotional rejection". The feeling is experienced when you keep reliving the social pain and disappointment about not achieving something that you desired. That is what happened to me when I experienced the death of a dream, relationships and unfulfilled expectations. They can make you feel like you are a failure. I experienced years of anger, bitterness, retaliation, depression and lack of confidence. Rejection has a way that compromises the quality of a person's life.

Everyone handles rejection differently. Thank God it didn't go as far as it could have, but it did affect me very deeply. The quicker you can identify your emotions determines how quickly it will be to accept them, change it and move forward. I wasn't aware of the negative beliefs and coping mechanisms that I had developed from the combination of my experiences that had become a part of me. So I based my reactions on the subconscious beliefs that I had about myself. I would try and protect myself from further hurt by being hard and telling myself, "I don't care" while disconnecting emotionally. I had and still have a difficult time trusting people because when I did open up, I was judged and misunderstood so I shut down and tried to deal with issues on my own.

Rejection also comes from neglect and seeks to destroy your self-esteem. You feel like you are never accepted for being yourself because some people just can't handle your issues. Although rejection hurts, I couldn't let it hold me back any longer. I had to come to the conclusion that there is a better way to look at rejection that eventually began to help me. I had to acknowledge my emotions and what I was feeling because "your place of truth is your place of healing and deliverance". Once you can identify what you are feeling, you can begin to heal from it. I had to change my viewpoint of rejection and stop allowing it to define me.

Rejection is what happened to me, but it is not me. In other words, I am not my mistakes, shortcomings or failures. I am who God says that I am. I have to treat myself with compassion and not be so hard on myself because of what happened. We are our own worst critic, and we are more apt to amplify our shortcomings and silence our victories. That's wrong. I have to speak positively to myself about myself and trust in God and his word to be my strength during the process. I have to recognize my true value and know my worth. I learned from Author Devon Franklin that when negative self-talk takes over, it drives you in a direction you don't want to go. I am a witness to that. I have to pray and walk in peace and confidence in the areas where I still feel insecure and rely on him. Things and people will let you down, but God never will. I have done wrong so many times but his grace and mercy continue to keep me and love me into wholeness and acceptance.

As I was going through my process I had to look back and ask myself, "What have I learned from all of this"? There is always something God is trying to teach us about ourselves. God wants us to not only be healed but made whole, so we don't keep repeating the same mistakes. As you go through your process, receive the love, acceptance and healing power of God. Allow it to transform you and bring the restoration to your life that you have been so desperately desiring.

The Start of My Transformation

Finding my way to my authentic self has been a journey. Over the last five years, I have come to learn so much more about myself than ever before. Trying to understand someone you've never known can be quite difficult and extremely emotional. When I think about transformation, butterflies are most commonly used as my point of reference.

Humans and butterflies are a lot alike because we both go through a metamorphosis to become who God created us to be. When you look at their life cycle, they undergo several stages before they become a butterfly. Life is about evolving and becoming and each one of those stages is necessary to our development. When I look at my life, I have evolved and matured through these stages several times to get where I am today. Just like the butterfly, struggle is necessary for me to grow. No one evolves overnight. It can take almost a lifetime to come into the essence of your being. It is something about the test, trials and struggles of life that helps build character and integrity, strengthens weak areas and makes you stronger for the journey ahead. Butterflies have to struggle inside of the cocoon to strengthen them for life ahead. If they come out of the cocoon too soon, it causes them to be underdeveloped and weak. It takes a combination of good & bad, ups, downs, tears, laughter, test and trials, setbacks and victories to transform us, mold and shape us so we are stronger, wiser and better for our purpose.

We all have a tendency to complain about our struggles but it is just the start of your transformation. How you see yourself at this present moment is not who you really are. But all that you have been through and will go through will help you come face to face with your authentic self. Our struggles have a way of helping us to find out who we are and what God said about us. It can take a lifetime to find out the "YOU" God created.

Pressure tends to bring out the best in you. We won't operate on our highest level by staying in our comfort-zone. When we find ourselves in these tough places, we should ask God, "What are you trying to perfect in me through this situation"? "What are you trying to get me to see in this situation"? God, give me a revelation of who I am and help me evolve and come forth with fresh insight on who I am becoming. Let's say hello to the new me!

I heard Pastor Touré' Roberts say something so profound and it really resonated with me. He said, "We will spend more time finding out who we are not, in order to find out who we really are. Everything you have been through and experience shows you who you are and who you are not." A lot of times we are embracing a false sense of ourselves. We embrace what people and experiences tell us about who we are. However, no one is capable of telling you who you are because they didn't create you. God did. So, we must pray and ask, "God, what did you have in mind when you created me? Help me understand who I am at the core of my being." To hear his answer, you have to let go of your expectation of how you thought life would turn out and flow with God.

It's all about evolving, or "*becoming*" as I would like to say. It's about telling yourself, "Self, I am about to run into who I really am.

How Do You Heal?

There is no other way I could begin the healing process other than looking to the word of God for strength, peace and hope. I never stopped attending church or lost my relationship with God because I realized that I could not do this by myself. When I talk about healing, I am talking about being delivered from deep-seated issues that I dealt with for quite a bit of my life. Some days were better than others. Some days I could feel the strength of God telling me I can make it. Other days I felt weak and like I just wanted to give up and give in. Our flesh will get tired in the fight of life but we've got to find the strength to keep moving forward. There is a lot riding on me to overcome my emotional battles because my decisions affect more than just me. Everyone that needs to hear my testimony is counting on me getting this thing right. However, when you've had cycles and bad habits for over half of your life, they don't break off that easily. Healing and wholeness will come, but there is a process to it.

To renew your mind you must change what you say to yourself and guard your heart and mind from anything contrary to what God says. It was in the area of my emotions where I needed the breakthrough that would bring me healing and wholeness once and for all. God has a way of repeating situations in your life until you gain the victory over them. He allows things to come to the surface just to let you see that you don't have it together like you think you do. I learned that I have to always trust God and rely on him no matter how much I think I have a handle on things.

Having the Right Perception of Yourself

When you develop the wrong perception about yourself it is the breeding ground for low self-esteem, doubt and insecurities to arise. You begin to question yourself and think that something is wrong with you, but nothing is wrong with you. It is a lie. Satan's number one job is to keep you from knowing your true identity in Christ.

He started early in my childhood, making me second guess myself and my abilities. He sends people into your life who speak words of negativity and do things to distort how you see yourself. He messes with your mind causing you to lack confidence in yourself. This is a never-ending battle because from the time you wake up to the time you go to bed, you are constantly fighting those thought patterns that are trying to nest in your head. But don't let the thoughts win.

It is so important to have a healthy self-image and to know that when God created you, you were fearfully and wonderfully made because you were created in his image and his likeness *(Gen 1:26)*. So how does self-image work when you don't *feel* fearfully and wonderfully made? When you don't feel good about yourself or don't like what you see? Ask yourself, "Where did these thoughts come from?". One word… PERCEPTION.

Our perception shapes our reality and is based off of a collection of our experiences. If not viewed properly, can taint every other experience in your life. Everyone perceives and approaches life differently. We have allowed society and what people have said about us to shape how we feel about ourselves. Since I don't look like what the world views as beautiful, then I must not be beautiful. Since I don't have what everyone else has going for them, then I must not be successful. We make the mistake of comparing ourselves with others and how they feel about us. I allowed what was spoken over me, what was done to me and how others felt about me to determine that I was flawed. I took the bait and it took my life down a path that continually left me emotionally depleted. Oh, I looked like I had it all together from the outside, but I was broken and hurting on the inside. All because of what someone said or thought about me. But the truth is that it's not what someone else thinks about me. It's how I see myself. I believe that that is one of the big problems that women have. We tend to put a lot of stock in what another human being thinks of us for our happiness. That is giving them too much power over your life. I have no right to expect anyone to make me feel good about myself. That is my job. So, I began to ask myself some tough questions and was shocked to find out that at the core of my being, I had the wrong perception about myself.

I began reading a book called *Exceptional You* by Victoria Olsten. There was a part of the book where she talked about a memory box where a lot of her family and friends put kind words about her into this box for her birthday. Whenever she would get discouraged about things going on in her life, she would go to that memory box and read all of the encouraging words everyone had written her, and it would lift her spirits. I don't have a memory box, but I did decide to follow Mrs. Olsten's pattern but with my own little twist. I decided that I was going to begin to see myself and my life with new lenses. I decided to focus on my victories and not my mistakes. I had been so stuck on what hadn't gone right in my life, what needed to be changed and not feeling worthy of God's blessings that I couldn't see straight.

It wasn't until I began to have a different perception about what I had been through, that I began to feel a little better each day. No, my situations had not fully changed but how I perceived them had. I began to focus on how far I had come and although I was not where I wanted to be, I thank God I was not where I used to be or somewhere much worse. God wants the change to take place in us first before seeing the manifestation outwardly. Any change that will be made in your life must first begin with a change of mind. Once your mind changes, the rest of you will follow. So, my prayer is that God would give your eyes to see yourself properly and to help you view your situations through the right lens.

Broken but Still Valuable:
The Importance of Self–Love

One day, I came across a social media post by Ty Tribett. In the illustration, he asked this young lady if she wanted $20. She said yes. He took the $20 bill, folded it, stepped on it, threw it and asked her, "Do you still want it?. "She said yes. He balled it up, he took it and unfolded it, stepped on it, and when he finished, he asked her again, "Do you want the $20?. When he finished the illustration, that $20 bill had been through so much, but even after all of that, it was still a $20 bill. The point I want to make is that no matter how damaged the bill was, it was still valuable. Like many of you, I thought that I was no longer valuable to God, to others or to myself because of all that I'd been through. I later learned that my value and worth would come from within. This sense of self-worth should be cultivated and nurtured at a young age, but many children like myself lacked that growing up. It is still no excuse to not try to develop it.

Love, of course, comes from God. He tells us in Mark 12:30-31 to love the Lord thy God with all thy heart, soul, mind and strength, and then it tells us to love our neighbor as ourselves. You can't love others until you first love yourself. Real love starts with YOU. It starts with identifying and loving who you are from within. If you don't, you will be running around being defined by the labels of others. We don't take the time to allow God to tell us who we are and to identify with that. We believe more of what society says about us. They will always devalue who you really are. That is why it is so important for you to love yourself.

After going through all of my disappointments, I decided to choose me and choose me first. I stopped looking for love and value from someone else and decided to start giving it to myself. While others around me were focused on being in a relationship with a "boo", I chose to go back to ground zero and find me. I wanted to master being a "whole individual", before getting into another relationship. It is so important to have a sufficient amount of self-love because the love that I have for myself helps to regulate what I accept from others and teaches me how to love and treat others. My love for myself lets people know how they can treat me and what I will or will not tolerate from them.

I will be transparent for a moment. I mentioned earlier that in my past relationships, I allowed men to place me second, while other things and people were first place in their lives. Then I would become frustrated and mad because they never made me a priority. Looking back, I realized that I didn't even make myself a priority, and while I desired and felt I deserved to be first place, I allowed second place to become my "norm". I settled with it for many years because I felt that it was all that I could get.

In late 2019, I felt like Ezekiel 37, when he was led into a valley of dry bones. As I looked around, I saw bones that were very dry in my life. What I equate the "bones" to were situations in my life where I felt hopeless, frustrated and disappointed. I just couldn't seem to make any sense out of where I was in my life. Once again, I was dealing with more unresolved issues and wondering how I can get out of this mental and emotional state. Then the Lord said, "Can these bones live? Do you believe I can turn your sorrows into laughter and your tears to joy? Do you believe I can go all the way back to your childhood and heal everything that happens to you and give you the life that I destined for you? In response, I said, "Lord, only *you* know. But today, I am beginning to see the light at the end of the tunnel." It may just be a flicker of light for me right now but at least I can see it.

Today, I am focusing on my value and worth that I have internally for myself, independent of anyone else. This is the time where I think that a little selfishness is OK, because many people feel guilty about loving themselves. However, it is necessary to have a healthy balance and respect for yourself. It's time to fall in love with you. Put yourself first and focus on your dreams. Consistently validate yourself with words of encouragement on your journey of self-love. Create a journal and meditate on affirmations that affirm who you are in Christ. Look in the mirror and tell yourself, "I am great. I am beautiful. I am powerful. I am extraordinary."

Whatever you need to do to stay on this path, I suggest that you do it. I would be remiss if I didn't tell you that as soon as you begin to put these things into practice, all of the enemies of your past will try to arise. When they do, you must choose whether or not to receive it. You must watch what you say to yourself when you are by yourself. Watch what we think when we are by ourselves. You must rid yourself of those thoughts sitting in your system waiting to sabotage your peace and happiness. Lastly, create a place of internal self-esteem where you build yourself up in God and his word over your life. Once you find that place, be sure to protect it and guard it and you will begin to see how loving yourself will make all of the difference in your life.

Staying the Course

"Brethren, I count not myself to have apprehended. But this one thing I do, forgetting those things which are behind, and reaching forth unto those things which are before, I press toward the mark for the prize of the high calling of God in Christ Jesus". (Phil 3:13-16)

We all have gone through difficult moments in our lives. Some are too painful to revisit. But nevertheless, out of those experiences, we have learned a lot about ourselves *(at least I hope you have)*. There is so much more to us than we can see, but it seems like challenges, disappointments and struggles are the things God uses to show us just how strong we really are. He lets you see that no matter what tried to break you, it couldn't, because He, our faithful God, is in us.

Any time that you start a new chapter in your life it will require that you do some things differently. As I started this chapter with a very well-known scripture, I am reminded of one who runs a race. Her course is already set up for her and her goal is to reach the finish line before all of the other runners. As she focuses on the race, she cannot let her mind go back to what happened in the last race she had run or who may be faster than she is, or what other runners did to prepare for the race. She has to put all of that behind her and concentrate on what is ahead. Life is a race and every fiber in your being must be intentional on two things: One: forgetting and Two: pressing forward.

There were a lot of obstacles that I had to push through to get where I am today. Like Paul, I am in no way saying that I am an expert in all of this, but I have my eyes on a bigger prize that is set before me that I must get to. That is the goal.

What is your goal? Or goals? You should have at least one thing that you are working on every day and pursue it with passion. I understand that sometimes, life happens. And when it does, it can cause us to be distracted and lose sight of our goals. But we need to know how to get up and get back on track. And not just get back on track but how to pull ourselves out of those pits when the enemy of defeat tries to drag us back. Some things are hard to get out of but are definitely not impossible. I want to share some things that have been a tremendous help to me, to assist you through difficult times.

1. Find a Personal Relationship with God

Having an intimate relationship with God gives you the strength you need to continue moving forward. I never could have made it to where I am today if it wasn't for my relationship with God. He has to be your partner in every decision that will be made concerning your life. He wants to be the one you run to when things get tough and you are at your wits end. He wants to be the one you can share your deepest fears with, He wants to be the one who heals all of your hurts and dry your tears. He wants to be with you every step of the way and lead you into victory.

2. Know Your Value

When you value something, you make it a priority, you take care of it, and you treat it special and won't let anything happen to it. You must recognize how valuable you are. This is something I have to remind myself of because we have a tendency to put other people and things before us without having a healthy balance. You have to look out for yourself, not in a selfish way but in a way that does not diminish you. What is keeping you from seeing the value in you? Don't let what you have been through or what you are going through make you feel like you are not valuable. *Remember, your value is not in the things you possess. It is in who God put us on this earth to be.* Let your value not be based on the opinions of others but on accepting that you are a uniquely created being in the sight of God.

3. Knowing Your Worth… and Add Tax

You, my dear, are priceless. You should never be able to be bought. And never let anyone put you on clearance. At some point, we all struggle with how we see ourselves and knowing our worth. But don't lower your standards or allow anyone to treat you any kind of way just to have someone in your life. Bottom line is …. don't settle. You are worth the wait; you are worthy of getting what your heart desires.

4. Know That You Are Enough

I have gone through life in and out of relationships with people who made me feel like I was not enough. They made me feel like I lacked something. That I wasn't good enough the way that I was. When God created you and me, he dispatched us into this Earth with everything that we needed to be all he is calling us to be. People have a tendency to make us feel like we have to do something extra in order to be accepted, but that is not so. You have to know within yourself that despite what anyone else thinks about you, you are enough, just the way you are.

5. Give Yourself Permission to Be You

So many people don't give you room to make mistakes or allow you to have shortcomings. I give myself permission to be me. I allow myself to have a bad day, to have a tough moment and time to be human. Sometimes I feel we put too much pressure on people to be perfect or to be a certain way. Take it from me; it's ok to be yourself. In fact, that is the only person you can be is you!

6. Your Setbacks Are Set-Ups for Comebacks

I have had many setbacks in my life. One too many, if I should say so myself. What I learned as a result was that my setbacks set me up to come back better than I was before. I became stronger, wiser, better, healed and whole, all from things that I looked at as setbacks, distractions, failures and disappointments. I would never have become the woman that I am if those things had not happened exactly how and when they did. We tend to look at our setbacks as something negative, and they might be, but hopefully they taught you something about life and about yourself that you couldn't have gotten if you didn't go through it. So be encouraged to know that out of the ashes of despair, you can arise and move forward with great power and victory.

7.   Know How to Encourage Yourself

There are times on this journey where you will feel like you are out here all by yourself, seem like no one cares, nor do they understand. But It is in those times where you have to encourage yourself in the Lord. This is the one time where I give you permission to talk to yourself and tell yourself, "You are going to make it", "You can do this", "you can overcome this", "you will be better after this", "trouble don't last always", "I won't give up", "I won't give in". When those tough times come, you must strengthen your inner man with different ways of encouragement. I know for me, I rely on the Word of God to give me strength, in those weak and dark moments when I feel like I don't have any more fight in me, God infuses me through his word and his promises that gives me hope and endurance that better days are ahead. When the trials of life weigh you down, you must draw upon the strength of God to help you make it through.

8.   Know Who You Are

This is one area where I believe many women struggle. We don't take the time to know who we are. We need to stop competing against each other and love who God created us to be. We diminish our greatness because we are focusing on everyone else instead of finding out who we are. One of the enemies to our destiny is to keep us from knowing who we are. So, remind yourself everyday of who God says that you are, what he says you can do and who he says you will be.

9.   Don't Compare Yourself to Others

Boy, how I have made this mistake so many times. We get so caught up in this and forget that God has created us all different. He gave us all special gifts, talents and abilities to be able to fulfill our purpose here on Earth. And when we want to be like someone else, it is like you are saying to God "there is something wrong with how you made me". You must find the beauty and unique essence of who you are and embrace it. Focus on being the best you can be.

10.   Know that Love Starts with You

Many women don't love themselves. And that saddens me. I used to be a woman who didn't love herself. At the time, there were so many things I didn't like about myself because I was unhappy with me. As bad as I attempted to give love, I couldn't, because you can't give what you don't have. I had to realize that in order to pull myself out of that low place; I had to see myself as loveable and love myself. I had to know and accept that God loves me even when man rejects me. Even when people walk away, even when I don't get it right all of the time, God's love never changes, and it never fails. No matter what place I find myself in, Good or bad, he loves me. I could never earn it. All I have to do is accept it. And when I do, it helps me to love Him more and it gives me the ability to love others. But it first starts with me.

11.   Look Forward to What is Ahead

In every vehicle you have two main mirrors. You have a large front window and a small rear-view mirror. Which means that what is in front of you is so much greater that what is behind. I started this section with Philippians 3:13-16, which tells us to forget what is behind and reach to what is ahead. For so many years, I wasted time looking back on what happened to me and the pain it caused me. So much that I couldn't see this bright, new future that was ahead of me. We spend too much time focusing on what happened, what didn't happen, our guilt, our shame and our failures, that we miss precious moments of today. I want you to get excited about your future. You can't change the past. It's just that… your past. But-- you can change your future.

12.   Have Healthy Connections

After having my relationship with God in its proper place, I found it imperative to have healthy connections.

I am blessed to have several relationships, but in my crisis, there was one that really spoke into me and changed the trajectory of my life. God didn't create us to be an island, going through life all alone. He knows that even though we have him, we need one another. You need those people to tell you when you are wrong, encourage you when you are down, make you laugh in moments of sadness and celebrate your progress.

13.   Find Emotional Stability

I can't tell you how important it is to have a sound mind. In my book, *"After This-Breaking Barriers to Your Emotional Freedom"* I shared my self-destructive behavior patterns that caused me to stall, stop and get stuck in my life. I had to find that place of peace from within if I was going to ever move forward. I made up in my mind that I was going to get to the root of those toxic behavior patterns and learn how to make better choices to maintain a healthy mindset and develop a thriving lifestyle.

14.   Rediscover Yourself

When you have been through a lot, it's hard to find your way back to those places where you were the happiest. So how do you rediscover yourself, the person that you know you are deep down? Fortunately, we never actually lose that person, and, by learning to change some of your habits and replace them with new ones, you can reconnect with yourself.

15. Go After Your Dreams

I noticed that when I began to go after my dreams, it made me more hopeful that brighter days were ahead. There was less focus on what had happened negatively in my life and the pursuit of my dreams became the motivation I needed. I decided that life is too short, and I only have this moment to make a difference in this world and live our lives to the fullest. So, I say to you quitting is not an option. And neither is settling. Go after those things God has placed in your heart and when you do you will be able to share a gift that the world needs to see.

Nedra Ford

Final Thoughts

I am finding my way to a better me, learning how to enjoy life and create things that bring me peace. My journey is a day-by-day process. More of the authentic me is coming forth as I move forward. I found that old things had to be released to embrace the, "real me" that was hidden by disappointment, frustration and insecurities. I know that everything that I have been through up to this point was used to get me to where God is taking me. I realized that some people come to teach you something about yourself and help to develop you into who God has created you to be.

The test and pressures of life are not there to kill us but to make us better and to show us how strong we are. These experiences show us how we can *take a lickin' and keep on tickin'*. My advice to all who will read this story is to, "Never lose yourself". I know how badly we all want someone special in our lives but never forfeit your happiness, your dreams or desires to have it. The person entering into your life should enhance you and help make you better. If that is not happening, you may want to rethink going any further. I know that there are no perfect people and there are no perfect relationships, but we must stop wasting time and energy on trying to get someone to be who they are not. Let's make the decision today that going forward, we will no longer

put ourselves on the back burner to make others happy.
Happiness starts with you!

It is my prayer that from my story, you were able to find
the strength that you need to be able to weather any
storm that you will face. Although we don't know what
life will bring our way, one thing we do know is God
has given us everything we need to see us to victory. You
may have noticed that throughout the chapters, I have
never focused on outer appearance, because we are much
more than that. My story is about overcoming and
gaining strength from within. Ladies, we are more than
just our pretty smiles. We are strong, we are gifted and
we are able to do anything that we put our minds to.

MEET NEDRA FORD
(Biography)

Nedra Ford is a native of St. Louis, Missouri, with a Bachelor of Science in Marketing from Grambling State University. At an early age, Nedra recognized the power of journaling and how therapeutic it was for her. She would often jot down her thoughts and feelings to deal with issues she couldn't talk about. When a tragedy hit her life in 2002, she found that writing was truly the only way for her to express what she was going through. Later, she developed her skills by attending several writer's workshops to home in on her craft. She realized that out of her mess, God was giving her a message to not only help her to regain her value and self-worth, but to help others who faced the same struggles.

Nedra is intentional about the growth and personal development of women of all ages and looks for ways to raise awareness about the importance of self-worth and wholeness. Her mission is to inspire and empower women through a practical application of God's word paired with some deep soul-searching. From her personal struggles, she relates with women who have found themselves in self-destructive behavior patterns and insecurities that stem from broken relationships and unresolved issues that have caused them to stall, stop or get stuck.

Nedra is the authoress of *After This, Breaking Barriers to Your Emotional Freedom*, where she shares how applying biblical principles and soul searching can enhance your life. Her desire is to help women pick up the pieces of their lives after facing challenges, setbacks and difficult matters of the heart. By identifying these emotional behavior patterns, we find healthy solutions and make wiser choices in order to experience an abundant life the way that God intended.

Nedra's story is a testament that no matter how low life takes you, there is a God, who can put your life back together again.

www.ingramcontent.com/pod-product-compliance
Lightning Source LLC
Chambersburg PA
CBHW041922090426

42741CB00019B/3447